THE AMERICA OF MY DREAMS

A POLITICAL MANIFESTO

DOM SGAMBELLONE

iUNIVERSE, INC.
NEW YORK   BLOOMINGTON

The America of My Dreams
A Political Manifesto

iUniverse books may be ordered through booksellers or by contacting:

iUniverse
1663 Liberty Drive
Bloomington, IN 47403
www.iuniverse.com
1-800-Authors (1-800-288-4677)

Because of the dynamic nature of the Internet, any Web addresses or links contained in this book may have changed since publication and may no longer be valid.

ISBN: 978-1-4401-8147-4 (sc)
ISBN: 978-1-4401-8151-1 (dj)
ISBN: 978-1-4401-8150-4 (ebk)

Library of Congress Control Number: 2009938462

Printed in the United States of America

iUniverse rev. date: 11/16/2009

CONTENTS

INTRODUCTION

I am angry, I am frustrated, and I think it is time for changes—real changes.

For many years we have all been brainwashed that we can only have two parties. Take one or the other. I beg to differ. There is room for one more. I have reached a point in my life that I can honestly say that I have lost faith in our current system. I, and I suspect many of you, feel disenchanted, betrayed, humiliated, and very badly manipulated. For the last forty-five years I have been just an ordinary citizen, an average citizen, who has been observing the country sliding down the proverbial tube. The damage done to this country, as I see it, was done not by foreign powers—not by outside forces—but the sheer corruption we have at all levels. Our political leaders talk about the power of hope and the need for change. What real changes has anyone seen lately?

I'm not claiming to be an expert. Other than some business reports, I have never written anything. I am not a professional writer. All I have is my lifetime experience, like many of you. Since 1975, I have been involved in corporate life—in management, financial management, accounting management, auditing, and all kinds of corporate tax matters. I believe that the real life experiences I have had make me qualified to offer some alternatives and at least give people something to think about.

This manifesto was written to make people aware of what the problems are and what we, the people, can do to stop the demise of America, clean the slate, and bring about real, meaningful changes at all levels: local, state, and federal government. We have the power to act, and act we must before it really is too late—before our country is sold off piece by piece for a fat fee.

What follows is a compendium of ideas and suggestions made by me, a man who is only known by his family and friends, a man with no political ambitions of any kind. I am not seeking office. I do not profess to be a legal scholar or a professional politician. I am, however, a citizen with an average education who, for the last four decades, has been witnessing the steady demise of this country. In the sixties this country was the land people dreamed about. Employment was good; integrity was a virtue, not a rare thing. People and companies seemed to be honest, and most everyone put the country first. Then it started: Special interests landed in Washington and started chipping at the system. They corrupted our system by buying our politicians with cash and lavish perks. These special interest groups do not have my interests or yours in mind. They are there like satanic creatures lining the pockets of everyone in Washington with money, gifts, vacations, etc. I am sure you get the picture.

Given that hell is going to freeze over before Washington fixes itself, it is up to us, all of us, to do the fixing by peacefully revolting and demanding changes from top to bottom. The first thing to do is to create a new and pure political party, one which really represents the silent and abused majority. This must be the birth of:

THE AMERICAN PEOPLE'S PARTY

For the longest time we have been led by our egregious politicians to believe that the Democratic Party and the Republican Party are the only viable political parties we can have. Nonsense. We can have as many parties as we wish. We have seen the Libertarian Party, the Green Party, even the Communist Party. So now it is time for the American People's Party. Not because we really need a new party, but because the Republican Party has become one of the rich, for the rich, and has lost touch with people. It therefore can no longer represent the interests of the average working stiff. The Democratic Party has tilted so much to the left that it would be better if they renamed it the Socialist Party of America. The ideology has now become some kind of mantra that preaches taking from the rich and giving it out to special groups and those who do not like to work.

This new party needs and welcomes anyone who loves this country, disenchanted members from all other parties and every walk of life. It needs people in all fifty states and at all levels. It needs leaders, activists, professionals, and volunteers. We must create this new and pure political entity all over the country and eventually nurture it into the party of the silent majority, which will truly represent the wishes of the American people. This new political entity must initially deny the majority to both the Democratic and Republican parties and eventually gain the absolute majority at all levels of government. This novel idea is not going to sit well with the entrenched establishment, and I am sure that many will attack these ideas and every one of us who share and support this revolutionary concept. Changes are scary, but everyone must remember the aim is not to do harm to anyone but to take back our country.

OBJECTIVES

The objectives are quite simple, and they are as follows:

Create a new political party called The American People's Party. The American People's Party must be activated at all levels: local, state, and federal. The new party must get the majority at the local and state level and especially at the federal level so as to be able to implement its new political agenda.

Achieve the majority of votes in city councils, state legislature, and the Senate. Change the present political mess into a monocameral system so as to streamline the legislative process, eliminate waste, and throw all dead weight from Washington and state legislatures.

Change the way candidates are selected. Eliminate the electoral system and modify the election method.

Change the way the Senate operates and how senators are chosen. Change all states' legislatures and executive branch so as to give more powers and more control over the state's affairs to the state.

Change cities' charters and change the roles of mayors, taking away some of the powers they now have.

Address the status of the United States as compared to the rest of the world.

Address current problems that are plaguing the United States, such as illegal immigration.

SUMMARY

The purpose of this summary is to give a broad overview of the objectives. Later we will explain, in simple terms, the various ideas.

FEDERAL ISSUES:

Amend the United States Constitution and achieve the following:

Merge the Senate and the House of Representatives into one legislative body—the new Senate. In other words, convert the existing political system into a monocameral system.

Change the method by which presidents are elected.

Change the way senators are elected.

Change the structure of the Supreme Court and the way justices are chosen.

Election of judges and the court system

Clarify and/or change some of the language in the Constitution.

The taxation system

Social Security system

Economy and finance

Foreign policy

Other federal issues

STATE ISSUES:

Amend the state constitutions in the following areas:

Merge the state senate and the state house of representatives into one legislative body and change the system into a monocameral system.

Election of governors

Election of state senators

The state supreme court

The educational system

The police department system

The fire department system

CITIES AND TOWNS:

Amend city charters in the following areas:

Election of mayors

City councils

Municipal taxation system

Municipal services

Other municipal issues

SECTION I –
THE CONSTITUTION

The Constitution of the United States of America was written by the blood of our forefathers. Many gave their lives to have a free country of the people, for the people. That idealistic dream appears to have died as crooked and corrupt politicians have hijacked the Constitution and changed its purpose, its meaning, and its original objective.

For the most part it is still a great document. It is also a document, which, over the years, has been twisted, used, and abused by the many groups seeking to advance their ideological agendas.

Even the current nine misguided Supreme Court justices have, for years, tried to read into the Constitution words that are not written anywhere. Every so-called constitutional scholar has tried to interpret what the forefathers meant. I say that the founding fathers wrote down in simple English what they meant. I do not believe that those men thought that if something was missing, some day justices would try to interpret what they meant. What they wrote is what they meant. They assumed that if something was missing, we would correct it without bickering over what the forefathers' language could be stretched to mean. If it is not written in the Constitution, it is not there. If it is not there, it must be inserted now so as to make sure there will be no doubts as to what it says. This will ensure that the will of the majority, the will of the neglected and abused majority, is the guiding light in our society. The Constitution is not cast in stone, and our forefathers, whose sacrifices and blood are still fresh on the document, recognized that and prepared for it.

In 1791 the states ratified ten amendments to the constitution. And why did that happen? The answer is that our forefathers realized that the original document could not possibly cover everything, every facet of life. The founding fathers were human and accepted the fact that some modifications were needed to deal with the changing times, thus the first ten amendments.

In these present dangerous times, with the whole world systematically turning against us, I find it necessary that some drastic changes take place in our society. However, I'm not advocating a blind revolution. Constructive changes are good; reckless changes are not. Changes to advance one single agenda at the expense of all others are not good, nor are changes that throw away over two hundred years of hard work for one misguided purpose. This country is still the destination of many people, and it should stay that way for the next century and more. It is for that very reason that I recommend the changes detailed in this book—to make this country a just and welcoming place for all its citizens.

Section II –
Merger of the House of
Representatives into the
Senate

This proposal, drastic as it may seem, must be approached in a businesslike manner. I am sure that everyone has heard of mergers and consolidations of companies. Banks do it, and businesses in general do it. When it happens, one also hears about the efficiency, synergy, and cost savings mergers bring. In this day and age where everything seems to be going out of control with our government growing bigger, more fragmented, and more expensive by the day, it seems to me that merging the Senate and the House of Representatives makes a lot of fiscal sense. Such an event would streamline the government, make it smaller, more efficient, and a heck of a lot less expensive than it is today. Just imagine the savings of sending home just about two-thirds of useless free loaders. The synergy and the effectiveness that it would bring would be priceless.

Our present legislative bodies are the Senate and the House of Representatives. The Senate is made of one hundred senators—two from each state. The senators are elected for six-year terms and can hold office until they die, literally.

There are approximately 436 congressmen in the House of Representatives, and these are elected to two-year terms and can run indefinitely.

In the case of the Senate, we now have very powerful and influential senators that have been in office, it seems, forever. As time goes by, these senators build very powerful political machines in their states, and unseating them is next to impossible.

It seems that the purpose for which they're been sent to Washington has been forgotten. The welfare of these senators comes before the rights of the people. As a result, people are very apathetic about the political process, and every six years they seem to be left without a real choice. Some senators even run unopposed. This is what our so-called democratic system is delivering to us now.

In the case of the House of Representatives, it looks like the congressmen are constantly running for office. They are elected for a two-year term, so as soon as they get in, they start planning for the next election. For the duration of their two years in office, they get ready for the next ballot while their duties and responsibilities are put on the back burner. These so-called representatives of the people are nowhere to be found when crises emerge or when critical issues surface. They are more interested in making sure that they take care of themselves and their cronies. They will make pacts with the devil to get what's good for them. There are some exceptions, of course, but those are few and far between. One might wonder how many representatives get into office with an average amount of assets but later seem to acquire wealth beyond comprehension. Hence the need for some radical reforms. The merger of the House of Representatives into the Senate would bring tremendous savings and benefits to the country. Here is how I envision it would work:

First, I would change the Senate term to five years. I would put term limits on the Senate to no more than two terms or a maximum of ten years in office. This would ensure that the people can actually bring about changes and bring in new blood constantly. The requirements to be eligible to run for the new Senate would be as follows:

- The minimum age for the first term would be fifty (50) years, and the maximum age would be sixty-five (65) so that if anyone is elected at age sixty-five, he or she would potentially be in office until seventy-five, so long as he or she is mentally capable.

- Senators would be on the state payroll, as they are state representatives in Washington DC.

- The U.S. Senate would only provide adequate staff and offices in DC. The states would provide offices and staff if needed at home.

- Senators would be part of the Social Security system, and they would not draw a special retirement pension once out of office. Rather, they, like any other worker in the United States, would be eligible for a regular pension.

- Senators would have to abide to a very strict ethical code of conduct; they would be prohibited from getting any money, property, privileges, or gifts of any kind from private companies, domestic or foreign. The senators would be working for their states, and no conflict of interests would be allowed. Violation of this code would be sufficient to expel any senator from office.

- If any senator were to run for the presidency of the United States, he or she would have to resign the Senate seat and then run.

- In the event a Senate seat became vacant, for whatever reason, a special election would be held to fill the seat. Governors would no longer have the power to appoint someone. The people would choose.

- Senators could introduce legislation with no "pork" attached. Special state projects would have to be the responsibility of the individual states—voted on according to their merits and financed by the states.

- Senators would not be allowed to fraternize with anyone who might act as a lobbyist, as lobbyism would be legislated as a criminal act.

- Senators would now really work for the people—all of us—and try to do what is best for the country. No more corruption, no more grafts, no more shady deals, no more selling our country to foreign and domestic interests.

- To secure election in their states, Senate candidates would be permitted to receive individual contributions only from U.S. citizens and legal residents in the amount of no more than $5,000 per individual.

- The new Senate would need a simple majority to pass any bill, and the filibuster nonsense would be rendered illegal. Any and all bills would have to be voted on based on their merit.

- The new Senate would have its own president, one elected by the Senate in full session soon after the results of elections.

- The Senate president would be in line for the presidency in the event the president and vice president die or are incapacitated.

- The Senate president would have the authority to introduce a candidate for the Supreme Court when an opening occurs.

- The Senate would need a simple majority to confirm a Supreme Court justice candidate.

- No senators would be allowed not to vote, to abstain, or to vote "present." Three failures to vote would result in automatic expulsion, and a replacement would be elected.

- The Senate would be comprised of 201 senators—four for each state, plus one for Washington DC.

- The new Senate would have several committees along the same lines as we have now.

- The new Senate would have the power to impeach the president or vice president for reasons spelled out in the revised Constitution.

- The Senate president would cast the tie breaker vote in the event of a tie.

- The compensation of the new senators would be established by their own state legislatures, and it could vary from state to state.

SECTION III – THE PRESIDENCY

If you have followed the last few presidential elections, you must be still scratching your head wondering what happened. How, in a country like this, did we select a president the way we did? What country are we in and who is calling the shots? Certainly the voters, the silent majority, were not heard. The special interests were.

For starters, we have far too many elections and too long of a campaign. That much money coming in from so many directions could buy an election, and perhaps already has a number of times.

I have the distinct impression that my voice does not count, that the voice of many does not count, that the voice of the *majority* does not count. What counts are the backroom deals and the manipulated results that force us to choose between the lesser of two evils. What a way to elect the president of the most powerful country on earth. There are many people quite capable and willing to lead this great country; however, under the current system they will not even consider it. Can anyone blame them?

SECTION IV – THE PRESIDENTIAL PRIMARIES

I do not know who or when it was decided that New Hampshire must be the first state to cast the primary vote. In the words of a former president, one cannot win the presidential nomination without New Hampshire or without going north to kiss the ring of a few people at the local diner. Wow … Forgive me, but I am not impressed. That may have been fine a couple of hundred years ago when the population was small, but it is not fine today. In a country of over three hundred million people, a few chosen people in New Hampshire should not have the clout to powerfully influence the outcome of the primary election. That, my fellow citizens, must change and not because the citizens of New Hampshire are bad but because there are millions of other voters who would like to have something to say about who is selected to run for the presidency. By the time California and New York cast their votes, the primary results are already in the bag for someone, and the many residents of the most populous states in the union do not have much to say. That must change. The entire primary system must be changed. Here is my vision of the process.

- Any U.S. citizen from any party is eligible to run in the primaries, provided that he or she meets the following criteria.

- Candidates must be at least fifty (50) years of age and no older than sixty-five (65).

- Candidates must be U.S. citizens for at least twenty-five (25) years and hold only the U.S. citizenship. Those with dual citizenship would not qualify to run.

- Candidates may raise funds only from individuals who are U.S. citizens or legal residents. No money from companies of any kind, domestic or foreign. No free advertising by any media outlet of private groups would be allowed.

- All states would hold the primary election on the first Tuesday of May of any election year.

- Candidates would be allowed to raise up to $50,000,000 in funds each and could spend the money any way they chose.

- The campaign and fund-raising activities would begin in January of any election year and would end April 30 of that same year.

- All states would be casting their votes on the same day. A candidate who wins the simple majority of the states would gain the nomination for the presidency of the United States. The simple majority of the states would be twenty-six (26) states, with Washington DC being considered a state for this purpose.

- In the event of a tie, the candidate with the most popular votes would secure the nomination.

- Candidates would be required to participate in four live debates over questions asked by citizens selected at random. The moderators would only read the questions and make sure the candidates abided by the rules.

- On the first Tuesday of May of the election year, the nation would know who the nominees were and would send the rest home.

- No candidates that lost the nomination would be allowed to run as "independent" or under any other banner. They ran, they lost, and they must not interfere with the will of the people.

- If a candidate wants to run as independent or under the banner of any other party, the candidate must announce his or her candidacy and register by the end of January of the election year.

Section V –
The General Election

Now that the primary is over and the parties, the Democratic Party, the Republican Party, the American People's Party, and others, have selected their candidates, the campaign for the fall election can start in earnest.

Candidates who ran in the primary and won in their respective parties are now eligible to receive federal funds for their campaign.

- Each candidate would receive a total of $200,000,000, which he or she could spend in any way.

- No money from individuals or corporations or any other entities would be allowed at this point.

- If any candidates have money left over from the primaries, such funds would be deducted from the federal money being given to the candidates. This would ensure that all candidates spend the same amount of money.

- Free advertising by companies or groups of any kind would not be permitted.

- Candidates would participate in five live debates with questions from ordinary citizens selected at random.

- Personal attacks on candidates' families would not be allowed.

- If any media network, talk shows, or media outlet gives time to any candidate, all candidates must get equal time.

- Media networks would not be allowed to endorse any candidate, but rather they must stay neutral and let the people choose the president.

We have now reached the end of October and the campaign stops. This pause will give the people a short time to ponder all candidates and choose who to vote for.

On the first Tuesday of November the election would be held. While the election is in progress, no network or any news organization would be allowed to make predictions, poll exiting voters, or do anything that might influence the election results. Once *all* states have closed their polls, exit polling would be allowed, and the media could say what they wish.

At this point the count would begin. Any ballots that cannot be clearly read would be discarded. It is the voters' responsibility to make sure they cast a valid ballot and not leave interpretation to others.

Absentee ballots would be allowed only for people with a legitimate reason to be out of their cities or towns. All branches of the military, embassy and consulate personnel, and other government officials assigned to foreign countries, for example, would automatically be given absentee ballots. People who are out for vacation or for a short business trip would not be allowed to cast their votes. Some civic responsibility must be introduced into the process. The voting day is known well in advance, and people must work around that date if they want to vote and be heard.

The votes would now be counted, but the weight of the votes would be different. Our current system is based on electoral votes. What this means is that small states do not carry much weight. They are not very important. Only the big ones with a lot of electoral votes are the target of candidates. In the new system, each state would count for one vote, and the candidate with the simple majority of the states would win the presidency, with Washington DC counting as one state. The candidate with twenty-six (26) states would win the election. In the event of a tie, the one with the most popular votes would win. In the event that no candidate gets the required majority, or twenty-six votes (states), a run-off election would be held four weeks later between the two candidates with the most votes.

Finally the nation would have its president. This new president would stay in office for five years instead of the four allotted under the current system—the idea being that anyone needs a bit more time to prove that he or she is up to the job. Obviously the presidency would have a term limit of two terms or ten years, and his authority would be along these lines:

- The president would have the authority to veto any bill passed by the Senate. To override the veto, the Senate would need 120 votes.

- In budget matters, the president would have line-item veto power so that some things can be put aside and debated another time without freezing the budgeting process and pushing the country into a mess. Both parties have done that at one time or another.

- The president would be the commander in chief and would be the principal architect of foreign policy.

- The president would select his cabinet members, and all members would have to be approved by the Senate.

- The president would not have the power to appoint people to his administration without Senate approval. The so-called "czars" would not be allowed.

- The president must abide by all laws on the books. Violation of such laws would be grounds for impeachment.

- The president would not be allowed to conduct clandestine operations without the Senate's consent. If conditions warrant it, such consent could be given in secret.

- The president's privacy would be protected, and if any classified information were leaked by a senator, that senator would be expelled from the Senate. In matters of national security, state secrets and classified information must be protected. This would ensure that the discourse between the executive branch and the legislative branch would not be revealed.

- The president would retain most of the other powers held now.

Section VI – The New Senate

The existing Senate is made of one hundred senators, or two from each state. The term is six years and there is no term limit. What this means is that professional politicians will run forever—well, at least until they die. The Senate is now an exclusive country club. They have excellent benefits, good pay, and outstanding retirement benefits. They do not even have to vote or be there when a vote is taking place—something we commoners cannot even dream about. What a life. No wonder these politicians will do anything to cling to their office and avoid leaving the club. No wonder some will go into the Senate chamber in a wheelchair with an oxygen tank on the side.

The amended Constitution would have the following provisions:

- Candidates must be at least fifty (50) years of age and no older than sixty-five (65).

- One term would last five years, and the term limit would be two terms, or ten years total.

- Senators from each state would be on the state payroll. After all, they represent their states.

- Senators would be part of the Social Security system like every worker in the country.

- Senators would be provided an office and an adequate staff so that they could actually work. They would actually write bills or read them, unlike now when lobbyists do the reading and explaining at times or even the writing.

- Senators would be prohibited from abstaining from a vote. They would be prohibited from voting "present."

- Three failures to vote during any term would be sufficient grounds for expulsion from the Senate.

- If a vacancy occurred before the end of any senator's term, a special election would be held for a replacement. Governors would no longer have the power to appoint someone for any Senate seat.

- Senators would be expected to introduce legislation as they see fit, provided that no pork or special attachments are included. Each bill will have to be introduced singly and with no riders of any kind. Senators would not be in any position to blackmail a piece of good legislation just because some pork is attached to it.

- Two senators would be the minimum required to introduce a bill.

- Any senator who wants to run for the office of president of the United States must first resign the Senate seat and then run. No more runs and then back to the safety of a warm Senate seat.

- Senators would be prohibited to meet with any one who might be construed as a lobbyist as lobbyism now is a criminal offense. This way the senators would work for the people and not for special interest groups.

- Senators would automatically be expelled if found in violation of the anti-lobbyists laws.

- The Senate would have several committees as it does today. The new Senate would retain most of its duties, including the duty to impeach the president or vice president if necessary.

- The new Senate would have a Senate president, who would be elected right after the general elections by the full Senate in session.

- The new Senate president would have the power to break a tie.

- The new Senate president would be the third in line to succeed the president in the event that both the president and vice president were to die or be incapacitated. The new Senate president would have the power to call a special session in the event of an emergency or other circumstances that require a special session.

- The new Senate president would stay in power until the next general election.

SECTION VII –
THE SUPREME COURT

The current Supreme Court is made of nine good, but at times misguided, people who are frequently driven by ideology rather than the laws, or even common sense.

Every time a vacancy opens up and a new justice has to be named and approved by the Senate, the candidates become the target of character assassination, no matter what president does the naming. The reasons a new justice is being brought in is forgotten. Politics get in the way and the current Senate even manages to destroy a candidate without giving him or her the respect of a formal vote by the full Senate.

This country was built on laws; it is a country of laws, yet some justices practice political activism from the bench. Some have even suggested the need to refer to foreign laws. Foreign laws? Are we incapable of legislating good laws? Do we need to refer to foreign laws? Or is this political activism? Let's not forget that foreign countries, for the most part, do not really give a rat's tail about America. This must change, and all justices must apply our laws, our Constitution, and nothing else.

Here is my dream of the new Supreme Court:

- Candidates must have been judges for at least ten years prior to nomination.

- Candidates can be picked by the president of the United States or by the president of the new Senate or by both.

- Candidates can be grilled pretty much the way they are questioned now by committees that will not have to vote on the candidates. Only the Senate will have the responsibility of voting.

- Once the preliminary hearings take place, there will be two candidates for the position.

- The new Senate will vote on both candidates, and only one will get the nomination.

- The one with the most votes in the new Senate will be receive the position.

- Only the Senate can say no to a candidate, not any committee, and every candidate will be extended the courtesy of an up or down vote.

- The new Supreme Court would be made of fifteen justices.

- The Supreme Court would apply the existing laws in accordance with our Constitution.

- The new Supreme Court would not interpret any provisions of the Constitution; they would read and apply what is written, not what they think our forefathers meant.

- The Supreme Court will not accept any suits filed by special interest groups of any kind. The Court will only hear cases that have been in the system and were appealed to the high Court.

- All cases brought before the Court will be heard and a decision rendered.

- The term would be set up in such a way so that every two years one justice would retire and a new one would come along.

- The term of all Supreme Court justices will be one ten-year term.

- All candidates must be at least fifty (50) years old and not older than sixty–five (65).

- In the event of death or incapacitation, a new justice would be elected by the Senate for the remainder of the term of the judge being replaced.

I envision the new Supreme Court being brave and fair and unafraid to tackle hot issues, such as abortion, gay marriage, eminent domain, and others.

In the case of abortion, the court must have the courage to declare that life begins at conception and that even fetuses must be protected by the law. The notion that a woman can do what she wants with her body is flawed. We are not talking about a tattoo or a ring in the tongue; we are talking about a human life, a life that must be protected under the law. For those who do not want to be bothered with motherhood, I would suggest that they get some kind of sterilization, free of charge under a new health coverage. The same would apply to men who may be too immature to be fathers, do not have the financial means to support a family, or perhaps just want to have fun. In such cases, these men must get sterilized, and then they can do what they want, but do not be an accomplice to a crime. Unborn children must enjoy the full protection of the law.

The Constitution does not say anything about the case of same sex marriage. Can anyone imagine our forefathers thinking about that? Unlikely. This subject would have been foreign to our forefathers, and I would say that they, the founders of this beautiful country, must by turning in their graves now. Court! Be bold and declare that marriage is between a man and a woman, and leave it at that. If same-sex couples want to live together, this is still a free country; they can have a civil union, but let's not change the fundamental rules to accommodate the needs of a few, only for political reasons. Get politics out of this court.

Regarding the eminent domain issue, nowhere in the Constitution do I see that developers, or any individuals, have the right to take a piece of property from someone so that they can build a better piece of real estate. This has happened so that someone can get richer at the expense of others. This is shear nonsense and must be stopped. Eminent domain, to a reasonable person, would be invoked for the purpose of building a school, a hospital, a highway, or something for the benefit of all and not just a rich few. Get the politics out of this issue, too.

And then we have the separation of church and state. The first amendment says, "Congress shall make no law respecting an establishment of religion, or prohibiting the free exercise thereof."

This has been twisted and turned upside down over the years. Why is it that such simple language is not understood or accepted? The Court in this case, too, must have the moral courage to clarify the issue and unequivocally state that the idea was to make sure that the government would not impose any religion and that we, the people, are free to worship any deity we want. So why fuss over this? Just stick to its words and meaning.

Section VIII –
The Court System and the
Election of Judges

When it comes to naming judges to the bench, it is always friends of friends. Over the years I have come across judges who are incompetent, corrupt, or lazy—judges who make their own rules, abuse the system, and make a mockery of the system. Once I was involved in a case, and, after six long weeks in the courtroom and after the judge used the jury as an advisory panel, reserving the right to decide the case, he finally rendered a decision. The plaintiff was elated, having won the case. The following morning, the judge amazed everyone and reversed himself. I could never understand what had happened and could only speculate. We, as ordinary people, all have felt at one time or another that there is nothing we can do. These judges sit high and mighty on the benches, and some could not care less about you and me or doing the right, moral thing.

Here are some suggestions:

- Judges should be elected by the voters in a general election to a single term of ten years.

- All candidates must be at least fifty (50) years old and not older than sixty–five (65).

- They must be a state resident for at least ten years.

- In the event of an unexpected vacancy, a special election would be held to fill the seat.

- All judges must adhere to the laws on the books and in the Constitution. No legislation from the bench ever.

- Any judge found to be in defiance of state or federal laws will be removed from the bench.

- All judges must adhere to predetermined sentences as outlined by the legislature.

- The criminal code must be streamlined and clarified and expanded so that justice can be served.

- The so-called parole system would be eliminated; all sentences must be served in full.

- Intentionally killing a person, no matter what the circumstances, would carry a mandatory life sentence.

- The death penalty would be eliminated, but mandatory life sentences without parole would take its place.

- Treason and espionage would carry a life sentence.

- Leaking secrets or classified information would carry a mandatory ten-year sentence.

- The president would have the authority to grant amnesty from time to time for certain crimes.

- The new code and the new courts would take away as much individual discretion as is feasible.

- Laws from other countries would not be allowed in our system.

- Individual rights would be respected; however, in the case of national security, the rights of society would prevail over the rights of one individual.

- In complex cases, the jury system would be waived and a panel of three judges would hear and decide the case.

- In murder cases a three judge panel would hear and decide the case.

- In cases where the mandatory life sentence is involved, a three judge panel would hear and decide the case.

- Each state will have its own court system, but all states would have the same guidelines.

- Judges are not above the law, and any proven violation carries a mandatory expulsion from the bench, and a replacement would be chosen.

- Some kind of tort reform would be done so as to limit the number of cases and limit awards in lawsuits, too.

Section IX –
Clarification and Update
of the Constitution

The forefathers lived in simple yet dangerous times, yet they put together a document that transcends politics, or at least it should. Unfortunately this beautiful tool has been twisted, ridiculed, and modified to fit ideology. The Constitution was changed before, and I do not see why we cannot directly modify it so as to deal with the twenty-first century.

The bottom line is, either we do away with the Constitution and replace it with new and complete laws, or we amend it so as to remove any interpretation that fits various groups and ideology.

Here are my suggestions in modifying the Constitution.

- Modify it so that we have a monocameral system with the new Senate being the legislative body.

- Modify it so that each state receives one vote in the presidential election.

- Modify it so the entire legislative procedure is revamped and simplified.

- Marriage is between a man and a woman, and this must be the law in all states. Same-sex marriage will be prohibited, but civil unions will be accepted and recognized with all privileges and responsibilities applicable.

- Abortions are strictly prohibited in all states except for in cases of the child's illness, incest, rape, or when the life of the mother is in peril.

- Life begins at conception, and a woman must not have the right to kill a human being simply because it is in her body. A six weeks fetus must have the full protection of the law; after all, we are a nation of laws. If women do not want the burden of a child, then they can have a tubal ligation procedure free of charge. Men can avail themselves of a free vasectomy. By having these procedures available, the abortion issue would no longer exist.

- The first amendment. Freedom of religion, speech and the press, rights of assembly and petition.

- The Constitution states, "Congress shall make no law respecting an establishment of religion, or prohibiting the free exercise thereof; or abridging the freedom of speech, or of the press; or the right of the people peaceably to assemble, and to petition the Government for a redress of grievances."

This is the famous first amendment that is so often ignored or abused. Let's try to understand it. Some legal scholars might think me a fool for even suggesting that we could interpret it; nevertheless, the country is made up of a lot of people like you and me, not just the few who like the system the way it is because it fits their ideology.

It seems to me that the forefathers were quite clear. The government will not impose any religion. In other words, the government is not telling us that we cannot *have* a religion; what they are telling us is that they, the government, will stay out of our religious lives so we can worship anyone we choose.

With this in mind, I believe that to have a prayer in school, or other public places, does not violate this amendment. The prayer can be generic so that anyone can direct his prayer to his own God. This amendment does not say anything about school prayers, and that is one reason why we have a mess today. Agnostic people, or people who are not sure that there is a God, demand we take the word God out of everything. Atheists have gone to the Supreme Court and are trying to get God out of our lives. What I say is quite simple. These nonbelievers are a small minority, and they have the right to believe what they want, but I do not believe that our society has to change to accommodate them. I believe that the rights of society must prevail over the rights of one, or even a few.

Let's be forthright and make sure that the language in this Constitution of ours is crystal clear. With our current system, changing this would be a just a dream, but when the American People's Party gains the majority in the new Senate, it can be done.

Now let us look at the freedom of speech and that of the press.

It seems to me, a layman, an average person with an average education, that the forefathers wanted to make sure that all of us would have the right to voice our opposition to our government without fear of retribution. I do not read in the Constitution that desecrating the flag or publishing pornographic material is protected by this amendment. It is not. Just ask yourself this: In what way does publishing pornography protect you from government retaliation in political matters? This amendment has been beaten and abused to death by people with an agenda. Clearer laws are required to deal with today's issues.

SECTION X –
THE SOCIAL SECURITY SYSTEM

Sometime ago I was in the office of a lawyer friend of mine, and we got to talking about Social Security and how it works. As usual, I got a lecture about Social Security. I was reminded that Congress, in its infinite wisdom, did not establish Social Security for people to retire on. I knew that and didn't argue the point. Congress did what they thought was best at the time. The problem is that a large number of retirees depend on the measly checks they get to survive, and they are losing the fight. Let me illustrate the point and explain why I think the system is inadequate, highly discriminatory, and in need of change.

In 2009, working people pay a Social Security tax of 7.65 percent, which includes 6.2 percent for Social Security and 1.45 percent for Medicare. The company they are working for matches the amount so at the end of the year the total contribution to the system is 15.30 percent. The Social Security tax is capped at the salary of $106,000 per year, while the Medicare tax continues indefinitely.

Now bear in mind that according to the Census Bureau the median income in the United States is just below $50,000 per year. What this means is that at least half of the working population will never qualify to receive the maximum amount Social Security is allowed to pay. As things stand now, the maximum pension is around $2,300. Someone who has always paid the maximum tax will only get $2,300. This does not take into account that some of this income may be taxed again when filing individual tax returns. If an individual were allowed to invest what he pays and what the company contributes in the private sector, he would have enough to live with dignity, something that half of our retirees cannot claim. Another consideration is that those who qualify for the maximum pension, in all probability, managed to stash away some savings that amount to a significantly higher amount than Social Security. Those who earned below $50,000 per year and only qualify to get around $1,000 per month, in all probability, have no savings and must rely on the Social Security check.

Now let's look at what is out there outside of the Social Security system, designed to take care of people with various plans. We see the railroad employees' plan, we see the many union plans, the federal employees' plan, and the state employee plans. And let's not forget the plan designed to take care of our Congress.

My friend, the attorney was right. Congress did not intend to have people live on Social Security when they retire, but they sure took care of themselves first and their wealthy friends next. This is what I call blatant discrimination. Are our retirees second-class citizens? I think not. After all, they worked all their lives to make a living; they contributed to the welfare of our economy and certainly contributed to some folks getting richer. And now that they are out of the workforce, they are left stranded and humiliated and unable to take care of their basic needs.

If we as a society take care of our retirees and give them more money to live on, it would be a constant economic stimulus because these people would spend the money on food, clothes, and other everyday staples. This kind of inequity calls for a silent revolution and we must strive to get the following accomplished:

- Merge all existing plans into the Social Security system so that we would have one equitable system for everyone. Eliminate all union contributions to any other private plans as all union employees would be participating in the Social Security system.

- Charge the Social Security tax of 7.65 percent total, including Medicare, and require companies and government bodies to contribute 15.3 percent for a total of 22.95 percent to the system. In other words the individuals would pay one-third, and the companies would pay two-thirds.

- Lift the maximum taxable salary and tax whatever anyone earns.

- Assess a per-head tax to companies who have employees in foreign countries. The tax would be $10,000 for each person employed abroad and who took the place of an American worker in the United States, and pay that to a general Social Security fund.

- Retirement benefits would equal 65 percent of the average of the last three years' gross earnings with a cap of $7,000 per month.

- Tax the retirement benefits only for Social Security tax or 7.65 percent or whatever rate the new Senate deemed appropriate. Retirement benefits would be exempt from state and federal income tax.

- Streamline the personal income tax rate and simplify it. Tax the income at the end of the year at the following rates:

  (1) Exempt the first $25,000 for single filers and $50,000 for married couples with or without children.

  (2) Apply a flat 15 percent tax on the rest of the income, including capital gains and all other types of income.

The new Social Security system would include all working people, including members of the new Senate and all federal and state employees. This new system would allow people who reach retirement age to actually retire and make room for the younger generations to fill in the jobs left vacant by the retirees. Anyone working after retirement age would not be eligible for Social Security. One either retires or one works, not both as the system allows today.

Section XI –
The Taxation System

Over the years, I am sure we have all heard calls to simplify the tax code. These cries fell on deaf ears as powerful lobbyists made sure that their friends in the Senate and House did what they were told to do. In other words, our representatives sold us out for the benefit of a few powerful special interest groups. The people that took an oath to work for and represent us betrayed us. There are also those who feel that the rich must be stripped of everything so that the poor can be taken care of. The poor have always needed the rich for jobs, their livelihood, and the rich have always needed working people to run their businesses. In other words, the rich and poor need one another. If the rich do not invest, no jobs are created. I do not profess to be an expert, but it seems to me that a middle-of-the-road solution can be achieved for the benefit of all. First, though, a new simple tax code must be written and implemented. Following are some of the objectives:

- Combine all kinds of different incomes into one simple category—total gross income.

- Exempt the first $25,000 for single filers and $50,000 for married couples.

- Add an additional exemption of $5,000 for each qualifying dependent.

- Apply one flat tax rate of 15 percent on the taxable income. No need for tax shelters or gimmicks. Capital gains would be part of the gross income and subject to the flat tax rate.

- Institute a VAT (value added tax) on purchases of products. The rate would vary from 5 percent on items of low cost to 20 percent on luxury items, including appliances and automobiles. Food products and clothing would be exempted, as well as medicines and drugs. This kind of tax would appropriately tax those who spend more a lot more than those who buy basic goods.

- Retain the gas tax and use that only to finance roads and bridges and maintain the infrastructure.

- Retain the cigarette tax and use that toward health care only.

- Retain the liquor tax and use that toward health care only.

- Do away with the inheritance tax.

- Do away with any other kind of tax now in existence.

- Restructure the corporate tax so that all corporations would pay no more than 15 percent on taxable income.

- Restructure the corporation tax so that companies operating abroad and moving jobs overseas will pay a flat fee of 50 percent on all consolidated taxable income.

- Give all corporations operating within the United States a tax credit for job creation and job retention.

- Give all corporations an investment tax credit.

- Give additional tax credits for buying products made in the United States and for raw materials.

- Disallow excessive executive compensation on tax returns.

- Eliminate all kinds of stock options and warrants as all employees and executives would only receive cash for compensation and bonuses.

- Bonuses would be declared and paid only out of earnings and only if the company shows a real profit and not one that has been cooked in the books.

- Executives would be held accountable, and all companies would be subject to stricter auditing standards.

- All publicly traded companies would be subject to audit by a firm selected by and paid by the Securities and Exchange Commission (SEC). Under this new scenario, the SEC would select the auditing firm to do the yearly audit and a midyear review. The SEC would pay for such services, and, in turn, it would charge the companies for the fee plus a percentage for administration and other costs. The firm selected would audit for three consecutive years, after which they would be rotated. The SEC would be given new authority and would publish the audit report for all stockholders to see. All auditing companies would report to the SEC and take instructions from it so as to render the audit independent. The SEC would also require that accounting firms not do consulting. Consulting firms would still be allowed and would be hired by the company, but these firms would not be allowed to conduct audits of any kind.

- The SEC would require that all publicly traded companies submit quarterly and yearly financial statements pretty much the way they do now except that such statements would provide more schedules and details of operating costs so that average stockholders would have more information available.

- Disclosures would include the names of all board members and their compensation.

- Disclosures would include the names of the top managers and their compensation.

- Abolish all "short sale" trading of stocks. The stock market should be for investors and not for gamblers who manage to manipulate the stock market at the expense of the average investors.

- Make the SEC accountable to the General Accounting Office or to another entity set up by the Senate. In essence, everyone would be held accountable. No more Ponzi schemes of any kind, and if something like that happened, the SEC and its officers would be held accountable.

- Mutual funds and all investment funds would be subjected to the same audits standards.

SECTION XII –
ECONOMY AND FINANCE

I do not believe that anyone would be surprised if I said that the economy is now and probably will be in the tank for a while.

The reasons for our current situation are corrupt politicians, inept mangers, and a lack of laws that severely punish those who caused the mess. Our politicians like things the way they are. Why not? They cheat, they steal, they lie, and their friends in Congress slap their wrists and that is the end of it.

The U.S. economy has always been somewhat shallow and susceptible to change with the slightest of problems. For example, the consumer confidence index goes up and down; the unemployment data, the housing data, profit reports, etc. are in constant undulation. These components have an effect on the economy and the stock market as well. Also ignorance on the part of the consumers in general hurts us tremendously.

Our economy has been fueled by consumer spending for the most part, but the problem is that, until the culture changes, it will continue to be that way. Most consumers live beyond their means. We all, at one time or another, buy stuff we do not need because it is on sale. We buy today and maybe will pay some day. Credit card use and abuse has been, and still is, one of the biggest problems facing the average person. The credit cards companies are so usury that, in another era, they would have been classified as loan sharks. Our politicians refuse to restrain them, however, having sold us out to the powerful banking lobbyists, and that is why I would like to see lobbyism classified as a criminal offense. There are steps that our leaders could and should have taken, but they do not think for themselves and must do what they are told to do. In return, they get money, power, perks, etc. The lobbyists are very powerful. They have money, time, and the gall to purchase our representatives in Washington, and that is why nothing gets done today.

Here are some of the steps we should take:

First, some industries must be regulated.

AIRLINES

Ever since the airlines were deregulated, one after the other has gone out of business or merged with others. The names of companies no longer in existence would fill a whole page. Deregulation was promoted as good for the consumers, but what about safety? What about having viable airlines that offer good service and efficiency? One should not have to spend a whole day in airports to get to a destination. I do not wish for airplanes to fall out of the sky piece by piece or run out of gas in midflight. This industry must be protected and regulated. Let the industry charge enough to make a profit and give a reasonable return to their shareholders and have this profit stop at a certain level. Anything beyond that would be taxed at 90 percent. Also airlines must be convinced to buy American-made planes. You see, when they buy Europeans planes, the competition is not on the same playing field. Foreign manufacturers receive subsidies from their governments and therefore can sell their planes at a lower cost than our manufacturers can. To compete with that, our government should provide incentives and tax breaks to our producers so that our people stay employed and so our people get the benefits of our airlines. In essence, the country should be on a buy-American track not only for planes, but for everything we need in our everyday lives.

ENERGY COMPANIES

Companies operating in the energy fields, including oil, gas, and coal companies, must be protected and regulated. Our national security may well depend on who controls them. For far too long we have been dependent on foreign oil. U.S. companies have developed the oil fields around the world, and because of that, we felt that we would have a reasonable supply of fuel, apparently forever. That is far from the truth. Local governments took over the oil companies and since then have been dictating terms of sale and even the availability of oil. They have set up a monopolist cartel so that they can gang up and set prices and production based on their greed. Their lobbyists have done a great job in Washington. The solution is not in finding out what we can do to get prices down; the solution is in becoming energy independent. We have enough resources and reserves to wave good-bye to OPEC and others and take care of our own energy needs. But here come the lobbyists and the environmentalists, people who could not care less if the price of gas goes up to ten dollars a gallon. These are people who are more interested in protecting the wild bears in the arctic than in protecting the welfare of the American people, particularly the middle and lower classes. My suggestion is to have a government of the people for the people. The American People's Party would accomplish that and do what is sensible.

I do not wish to ignore environmental issues, but I do wish that we could find a way to balance our needs with the needs of the bears and the caribous. Our government must commit to finding a way to eliminate oil dependency as soon as possible, which will help both the wildlife and the American citizens. During World War II, the United States committed resources and manpower to the Manhattan Project, and approximately 150,000 scientists managed to come up with the solution. This project was put together to develop the atom bomb that eventually led to the end of the war. In 1961 President John F. Kennedy committed the country to getting to the moon in the next decade, and we did. We can now commit to coming up with alternative fuels in the next ten years and becoming independent and much safer than we are today. Also, when the Alaska pipeline was first proposed, there was an enormous outcry. Twenty years or so later, the life of the bears and other wild animals has not changed. The same would be true if we were to drill for oil in the ANWR section of Alaska. We have the technology and the will to protect both the public and the environment.

We could also have automobiles run on natural gas, as we have plenty of it. There are some that will tell you that we do not have the technology. I would say that is nonsense. If our government demanded that the auto industry make adjustments, it would be done.

About twenty-five years ago I was in Italy with a friend and his family. It was a Sunday afternoon and we were going for a drive. When we stopped for gas, much to my surprise, we tanked up with natural gas. It was like going to get the barbeque gas tank refilled. A few minutes later we were on our merry way on the highway, and you couldn't tell that the car was running on natural gas. Why not us? Are the Italians smarter? Is the rest of the world smarter? Or is it that the oil companies' lobbyists are stronger than our government? You and I collectively can decide what the problem is and take action by revamping our political system, which is at the base of all problems.

So the energy-related companies must be regulated. They would be allowed to make a reasonable profit but not to take advantage of the consumers as they have in the past. A threshold of profit would be set, and if they go over that, the excess profit would be taxed at 90 percent. The same would apply to all energy-related companies.

PHARMACEUTICAL COMPANIES

These companies must be regulated, too. The cost of prescription drugs has gone wild, and many people, particularly our retirees, cannot afford them. If one compares the price of any prescribed drugs against the same generic drug, it looks like we are buying designer products. This is insane. Naturally, our government must allow this industry to make a reasonable profit, but anything beyond reasonable would be taxed at 90 percent. These companies could still avail themselves of all tax credits available to all businesses.

CREDIT CARD COMPANIES AND BANKS

If I weren't angry, I would extend my congratulations to all lobbyists who have managed to muzzle our politicians and essentially legalize stealing. You will hear that credit card companies must get more because of the risk. That is somewhat true, but given the fact that credit card companies give cards out like there is no tomorrow, one has to wonder if they really care who is holding a credit card. As it is, we have too many people who have used and abused the privilege of credit and gotten into a mountain of debt. If one figures the rate of interest to be somewhere around 30 percent, plus penalty fees, many people will never get out from under that mountain. So here is the solution: First and foremost, credit cards should only be issued to credit-worthy risks. Credit companies should extend a reasonable amount of credit, and the interest rate must not be more than five points above prime rate. In other words, the way the prime rate is now, the average consumer would pay around 9 percent interest. I would want to see this change retroactive to five years. The degree to which credit card companies are taking advantage of consumers is criminal and must be stopped. We the people can accomplish that, not the current politicians in our government.

Let us now look at the loan practices of banks in general. In the past, banks were so eager to put loans on the books that they forgot to whom credit was being extended. A banker friend told me once that they got out of the auto loans business because they lost about twenty-five million dollars. They were working with an auto dealership that was pushing cars to anyone. Once financed, the cars made their way south of the border, never to be seen again. The bank was then left with a lot of worthless papers. It seems to me that no one should be extended credit for more than 85 to 90 percent of what they buy. There are some promotions that push anything, including no money down or "buy now, no interest for two years" and so forth. This must stop. If any consumer wants to buy something, he must pay for it either in cash or over time if he is credit worthy. If banks do not do their job of investigating this at the beginning, then they should not come to you and me to bail them out as they have been doing recently. Let the banks make a reasonable profit, but let them fail if they do not know what they are doing. It is a simple concept, and investors should demand that anyway.

Industries aren't the only areas that need regulation. We need to look at our own buying habits. For example, we need to look at our reliance on foreign products. Just keep this simple concept in mind: any time we buy products made abroad, we keep employees working in foreign countries while our workers here are systematically losing their jobs. In years past, the notion of buying a product at a better price was accepted; however, when you see our manufacturing companies moving the majority of the jobs abroad, then we all need to start buying domestic products. I understand that sometimes the price is a consideration or the quality is an issue. But I see a lot of junk made overseas on the shelves, too. We can all help fix the economy by buying domestic products. Demand value and quality and make sure that our people, our workers, stay employed.

Unions might as well join the chorus and preach to their members to buy domestic regardless, whether the products are union-made or not. I would venture to say that if we all started buying products made or grown stateside, we would see our economy take off like a rocket. Let's not whine and start acting instead. Remember that every dollar that goes abroad is responsible for job losses here in our USA.

Regardless of where the product is made, we all, over the years, have bought items that didn't actually improve our lives. Stop that and think before you buy. Most importantly, buy only what you can afford. Nowhere in the Constitution does it say that everyone must have this or that. Happiness often comes from within and not from the acquisition of junk.

VACATIONS AND TRAVEL

And again there is traveling abroad for vacations. Many of us have indulged in making some foreign trips at one time or another. When we do, the money we spend outside of the United States is detrimental to our economy and helps the foreign country keep its people employed. Let's just make some changes. Let's vacation in this vast land of ours. This country has just about everything and lots to see, so let's put off our foreign vacations and do some travel to a region of the States we haven't seen yet. Take the opportunity to see what we have and what we must strive together to preserve. You may even better appreciate the country we want back.

WASTE

I believe that we, as a nation, waste a lot. We even waste the basics—food, clothes, and other staple goods. Some third-world countries could sustain themselves with what we waste. We can stop that by buying reasonably and limiting what we waste. Our consumer habits must be reassessed, and in doing so, we can push our economy to the stars.

SECTION XIII –
FOREIGN POLICY

First and foremost let us throw away the self-flagellating notion that we, the United States, are responsible for the world's ills. The people in other countries are responsible for the leaders they choose, and they, too, can bring about change rather than waiting for the USA to bail them out. No more bailouts for anyone. They, too, have the responsibility to take charge of their own destiny. And if they are not capable of doing so and need help, well, the Europeans or the worthless UN can assist. After all, they have proclaimed themselves equal to or better than us. I agree that they are equal to us, and now it is time they put their money where their mouths are. Talk is cheap and it is easy to criticize; now they need to show what they can do or what they are willing to do.

The same applies for the Far East. China is there—a rich China that could do a lot more than it is doing right now. Japan, Australia, and other Pacific countries could do more to enhance their own security or help less fortunate countries in the area. The USA can no longer do it alone, and most of all, the USA does not *want* to do it alone. World

War II is over. It has been over for more than a half a century, and it is time countries all over come to grips with that rather than being opportunistic and trying to sponge off the good old USA.

There are some in high places who profess that we are responsible for everything that is happening in the world. I heard someone once say that a big hurricane was the responsibility of the president of the United States. Nonsense. We are not at all responsible. As a reminder to everyone, we have invested money and lives for the freedom of millions of oppressed people, but memories fade and political opportunism obscures what this country has done for the entire world at one time or another.

We no longer have any real friends in the world, just allies of convenience.

The time has come for us to restructure our entire foreign policy along the following lines.

THE UNITED NATIONS

The beautiful complex in New York City overlooking the East River started as the League of Nations right after World War II. The intent was noble, but many nations could not afford the membership fees, so the good old USA footed the bill, or most of it. A wealthy New York family donated the land, and the famous complex of buildings and halls was built. Over the years, as countries grew, this organization became more and more hostile toward the United States. Today it does not matter what we as a nation did to make sure the world was free of tyranny. It does not matter that we did away with Nazi Germany or imperial Japan. It does not matter now that we poured billions of dollars of our tax money into Europe and the Far East to rebuild the countries. We won the war but they got our money—your money.

The intent of this organization is noble except that just about every aspect of this country club is corrupt to the core. The United Nations spends money like the proverbial drunken sailor. It's not their money, so splurge, and splurge they do. Let me say that money is no object when it comes to taking care of a lot of corrupt crooks.

First off, we must quit the organization that has betrayed the purpose of its creation and become a plush country club for useless "diplomats." This worthless club has also become a forum for any two-bit politician to mouth off and bad-mouth our USA while the rest of the delegates cheer on. You see, no one at the United Nations likes the USA. On the contrary, they hate us, and they are envious of our way of life and would love nothing more than to take us down even at the risk of losing a fancy office in New York. So let us quit the United Nations and evict them from New York City. Let the club relocate somewhere else. I am sure Europe would welcome it, so let Europe, Russia, China, and others foot the bill for this useless club. The benefits of such a move would be tremendous. First off, we would get our New York City back and save the billions of dollars we spend to support it and to keep track of all the spies that operate out of the United Nations with the cloak of diplomatic status. Most of all we would not have to explain what we do to this corrupt organization. Perhaps when we disengage from most of the world's problems, the rest of the world might appreciate what they've lost.

NATO

This alliance was fine in the aftermath of WWII and the presence of the former Soviet Union. Times have changed, though, and nations in this alliance are moving with the times in the sense that they do only what is best for them.

When the Soviets were lurking on the other side of the Berlin wall, no one complained about our presence in Europe and elsewhere. Our tanks were a welcome sight and our soldiers were respected. Things have changed. Russia is no longer an enemy. This can be argued, but who am I to contradict two presidents who made such a claim? Every country in Europe has its own problems and objectives, and because we do not share the same political views with any of them, our presence is viewed with suspicion and distrust. These European countries have convinced themselves that they no longer need us, and I agree with them.

So, given that Europe has matured and is free and rich, let Europe take care of its own needs. Militarily and economically Europe may not be at the same level as the United States, but when I hear prominent European politicians preach that Europe must arrive at parity with the United States, I say, let them. Let's get out of Europe and bring our troops home. Quit that organization and, if feasible, establish new alliances with nations that truly like us and that are willing to share the burden, both the financial and the human resource costs.

For some time now the Europeans have not wanted to share any military burden. They will contribute troops for training and administrative purposes, but not for combat. These elite countries forget that if the United States had not entered WWII, they would have a common language—German. Only the graves at Normandy, France, sometimes remind them of what we did. But their new generation does not care. Not only do they contribute little to the alliance, but in some cases they have been trying to undermine what we do and how we do it. They have developed this notion that they are smarter, wiser, and much more knowledgeable about European affairs than we are. I agree with that assessment and propose that we go our separate ways. We'll take care of our security, and they can take care of theirs.

Another thorny issue is the presence of our troops on foreign soil, in Europe, the Far East, and other places. Everyone must come to grips with the fact that WWII ended a long time ago and the Soviet Union collapsed some time ago. So why do we need to have troops in Europe or elsewhere, one might ask. I say we do not; therefore, close all bases in Europe and bring our men and women home. Let them spend their pay in the good old USA. The Europeans are strong enough and smart enough to take care of themselves in the event of trouble, and they can have their own alliances if they so wish. We do not want to be big brother when we are needed and an unwelcome guest when things are quiet.

In Japan, South Korea, and other Asian countries we are not wanted. They forget how much money we poured out to rebuild them after WWII and the Korean War, which, by all accounts, is still on. Both countries have matured and have plenty of money to fund whatever defense they need. Besides, what can 38,000 troops do against a million troops of North Korea anyway? The South Koreans can build their own army and take care of themselves, and if they cannot, let the United Nations come to the rescue. So bring our troops home. These men and women could help patrol the southern border and make sure that our new immigration laws are respected and that the border is safe.

At this point in restructuring, we will have brought our troops home, and the rest of the world will be left to take care of its own needs. I am sure some countries genuinely like us and would welcome an alliance with the United States. These we would consider case by case. While our presence on foreign land diminishes, we will maintain a very strong military force at all levels. We must continue to research and produce weapon systems so as to ensure that we have the technology and strength necessary to defend our homeland, should it be necessary. I would want a very strong navy and air force and certainly a strong army adequately manned to deal with any crisis at home or abroad if our interests and security warranted it. I would want to see the draft system reinstated so that everyone, including the liberal-minded boys and girls, would see firsthand that our freedom is not guaranteed and must be protected at all times. Any surplus of personnel could perform duties at the border or in cities and towns on a civil assistance basis in conjunction with state national guards. The tour of duty would be a mandatory eighteen months. It is quite simple to protest from a comfortable armchair, but it would be a good education for our boys and girls to experience something real once they get out of high school. In the words of someone more important than I, we must be ready for war if we want peace. Other countries are doing so even though they say they are not. In summary, we must have a strong army, a very strong navy, and an exceptional air force. We must also have a strong National Guard at the state level.

Section XIV –
Other Issues in Foreign Policy

There are a lot of other issues that could and should be examined, but I shall not dwell on everything, just some of the major issues. Part of our foreign policy is how we protect our borders and freedom.

The Borders

Particularly in the south, the border is very vulnerable to violation and open to abuse. People with good intentions and also those who would love to destroy our country have easily entered the country unnoticed. These uninvited guests roam the streets of our cities, protected by disobedient mayors and some governors and certainly many in Congress. If we are to believe what we hear, there are about twelve million illegal immigrants, and our cowardly politicians do not have the guts to tackle the issue. With the exception of a few in Congress, everyone looks the other way. Now there are those who preach that we must treat illegal immigrants like U.S. citizens and offer them a free health plan and other benefits. To many, it isn't important that hardly any of them pay taxes and therefore sponge off our system. They want more, and why? Potential votes. Hence the need to tighten our borders and protect this country.

Way back when, the Chinese feared invasion by the Mongols, so in order to protect their country they built the Great Wall of China. It took a long time to complete it, but it is still there after thousands of years. I do not believe that the wall was ever breached or even violated.

Nobody, in the last couple of centuries, ever complained about the Chinese trying to keep their enemies out. I am sure that building the wall kept many people working for many years. So, bravo, Chinese. They did what they thought was best to protect their country and interests.

The Roman Empire experienced something similar. When Emperor Hadrian's troops occupied England, the northern tribes were pushed north. The Romans feared that those tribes would, one day, come down and attack them, so the emperor decided to build a wall that virtually cut England in half. This wall was built for the sole purpose of keeping the Romans' enemies out and has been known throughout the centuries as Hadrian's Wall. In fact, it was not just a wall; every so many miles a village was built, too, with shops, trade posts, and other necessities. In these villages, trade prospered while the soldiers monitored the wall, keeping watch on who was coming and going. The tribes never really tried to knock the wall down; only time did that, and today part of the wall is there as a reminder that it was built for defensive reasons, not to keep the good guys out.

We now have a similar problem at our borders. In the south, the border is an open sore, and politicians are desperately trying to use that to score political points. Our safety and security is not that important: only politics is. A few good men and women have tried to tackle the issue just to see it muzzled in Congress.

I do not mind seeing immigrants come to the United States for a better life, but I want these good immigrants to come through the front door and not through the back door (or through a tunnel or over a fence). The United States has always welcomed people of all colors, creeds, religions, and aspirations, and many of them contributed to the development of this country. Now with a new wave of immigration, it is important that immigrants come in legally. Let us start by securing the borders. First off, let us deploy military forces along the borders, be it the National Guard or army units. Let these units patrol and help enforce immigration laws. We can also have civil units assist with the task. We can and must build a wall like Hadrian did. This may not be welcomed by bordering countries, which in some instances encourage their people to go north to the United States so they have one less problem to face. However, this is not their country; it is ours. We, and only we, have the moral and legal responsibility of protecting our borders, our country. Many politicians today would attack this plan. The way the system is designed today, if one party manages to legalize the many illegal immigrants that roam our cities and towns, it would get many more votes, or at least so the party members believe. Today California would get an additional nine representatives in Congress if the illegal immigrants were counted as U.S. citizens. On the other hand, if we modify the Constitution so that each state counts for one vote in the presidential elections, it would not matter if many more people were legalized, so the political nonsense would come to an end.

When it comes to immigration laws, everyone you hear has an agenda. Nobody really has the fortitude to face the issue and offer solutions. I would be doing a disservice to all if I did not propose what follows:

- Secure the border first.

- Mandate that employing any illegal aliens is a criminal offense subject to mandatory jail sentences of at least five years.

- Mandate that any employer hiring illegal aliens would also be subject to a fine of at least $10,000 per illegal employee.

- Mandate that any expenses paid by any employer for illegal aliens would be disallowed as tax breaks in their tax returns.

- Mandate that any illegal aliens apprehended in the country would be deported without a hearing, as aliens have no legal rights in the USA.

- Mandate that any money spent for the deportation or treatment of any illegal aliens would be charged to the country the aliens came from.

- Mandate that all workers in the United States must have a valid Social Security card and some kind of workbook, which must be issued in person after all documentation is checked and approved. Issuing false documents would result in a jail sentence for any Social Security administration employees.

- Illegal aliens would not be allowed to transfer money back to their country.

- Create a path to legalization for the existing illegal aliens. These people must be accounted for and given the proper scrutiny. Criminals or people with criminal records must be deported immediately. People with a clean background and who have lived and worked here for at least ten years would be given legal residency and green cards. They would also get a path to citizenship in accordance with immigration laws.

- A fee of $3,000 must be paid by each alien who wishes to get legal residency. Families would pay no more than $6,000. These fees would be used to cover the administrative cost associated with the legalization process.

- Mandate that anyone aiding illegal aliens to come to the USA would face a ten-year mandatory jail sentence, with no possibility of parole.

- Mandate that any mayors or public officials aiding and abetting illegal aliens would be subject to stiff fines, mandatory jail sentences, and immediate removal from office.

The problem must be fought on both sides of the border while shifting some of the responsibility to the country of origin that, as it seems, encourages emigration.

Another unspoken issue that might become a real problem in the future is, what are these illegal aliens doing to our country? Let me express a thought. According to some historians, when Texas was part of Mexico, a stream of settlers came from other parts of the USA and set roots there. Little by little this type of illegal immigration led to the formation of the Republic of Texas and eventually the annexation of it to the United States. The way I see it, we are risking the same problem in reverse. Perhaps that is the long-term aim of some. Unless we fix the problem now, we will have severe and costly problems later.

Section XV –
Affirmative Action

Affirmative action must come to an end, and good education must replace it. The intent and purpose of affirmative action was noble, but its usefulness and fairness is coming to an end. One must also keep in mind that in the United States we have many minorities: Latinos, African Americans, Asians, and Europeans. (Yes, people still emigrate from Europe.) And let's not forget our former landlords, the American Indians who still live on "reservations."

The time has come when people must get ahead and be successful on their own merits—because they are smart, because they work hard, and because they are dedicated to their profession. To accomplish this, in my dream of America I see an equitable education system so that everyone will have a chance at getting a good education and affirmative action can be gradually phased out. In my dream I see each and every state in the union taking over the education system in their states so as to put an end to the discriminatory system we now have.

Discriminatory, one might ask? Yes, highly discriminatory. Let's look at what we have. Each city and town has the responsibility to educate their residents. They fund the school system with local and real estate taxes. This means that wealthy communities get the best of the best for their kids, but poor cities and towns struggle to stay afloat. When states take over the schools and make the educational system equal for all, it would be the beginning of the end of this dichotomy. I dream of seeing state schools of the same quality as, or even better than, the best private schools. Bear in mind that I am not suggesting we close local parochial or private schools. They can still exist but without state or federal funds. Their benefactors or high tuition can still fund them; however, I do not see the quality of the education being better than that of the state-run schools.

In essence what we need is a good and fair education program to replace affirmative action. I want to see kids of every background, race, or color grow to be doctors, engineers, accountants, and lawyers without having to bankrupt their families. The tuition for secondary education would be very reasonable, roughly $3,000 per year to go to medical school or law school. The new state and federal tax system would finance our kids' education.

Section XVI –
The Health-Care System

Much has been said and not much has been done. Do we have a good health system? I think so. It is not perfect and it could use some improvements, but, for the most part, it is what the general population has and likes.

Some politicians claim that we have a messy system, one that neglects the uninsured and some minorities. I beg to differ. A very high percentage of citizens have health coverage, and they are happy with it. Some do not have insurance, and they resort to welfare, Medicaid, or other state and local programs. The system can be improved, so let me offer my thoughts.

- First and foremost, leave the system we have alone, but regulate insurance companies so that they do not take advantage of clients dependent on care.

- Mandate that any employer who has two or more employees must provide health insurance to them, and the cost to these employers must be reasonable. Small employers cannot be penalized because they have a small group.

- Mandate that employees can take the coverage with them if they lose their jobs or change jobs.

- Mandate that employees contribute up to 50 percent of the cost of insurance, but leave that to the employer's discretion.

- Establish state-owned and run hospitals and clinics along the lines of VA hospitals. In these hospitals no one would be turned away.

- Mandate that pharmaceutical companies contribute some drugs and medicines to these hospitals.

- Mandate that these hospital and clinics be funded 50 percent by the states and 50 percent by the federal government. States must bear some of the financial burden.

- Mandate that these hospitals and clinics are available to all, including those who have health insurance.

- Mandate that the number of students entering medical schools, state or private, be increased drastically so that the number of doctors would increase, thus reducing some costs. The student body will naturally increase on its own as the cost of medical school decreases.

- Mandate that graduating doctors from state schools work for at least one year at the state hospitals and clinics.

- Regulate fees so that there is some consistency from area to area. Doctors now charge pretty much what they want. It is a free enterprise system. I suggest that there be a cap for each type of procedure. State workers' compensation systems already have fee schedules in place, so health service providers will get paid what the fee schedules dictate.

- Mandate that the Medicare system be placed under very strict auditing procedures so as to root out fraud at all levels.

- Mandate that fraud in the Medicare or Medicaid system is a criminal offense with a mandatory jail sentence of at least five years. Doctors, hospital managers, clinics, or anyone involved with Medicare, Medicaid, or state-run hospitals will face a minimum of five years in jail if convicted of fraud. Let's stop the nonsense. The double billing, billing for services never rendered, and so forth must come to an end.

- Mandate that the General Accounting Office be the watchdog of all audits with the authority to hire auditing specialists from the private sector to monitor Medicare, Medicaid, etc.

- Mandate that the General Accounting Office reports to the Senate every six months.

We have a system; all we need to do is to improve it and make it so that everyone, including federal and state employees, is part of it. No separate or superior plans for the Senate or the president. Health problems do not discriminate, and all should have a fair plan regardless of financial means.

I learned, not too long ago, that the plan Congress has now is a very generous one. One that all of our representatives in Washington are eager to keep while pushing some kind of totalitarian plan for the rest of us. Let's make sure it does not happen.

Section XVII – Illegal Drugs

I do not believe that anyone really knows what the cost of fighting illegal drugs is. We have the coast guard, state police, and local police fighting this losing battle with no end in sight. This is the kind of war that produces corruption at all levels. Is there a solution to the problem? Here are some thoughts. We can use the funds we spend to fight the drug war to do the following:

- Proclaim that the United States will buy all drugs produced by anyone abroad. These purchases would be made legal so that everything would be on the up and up.

- Institute a policy to compensate drug growers to either grow something else or not to grow anything at all. Growing drugs in the backyard would be illegal.

- Institute a purchasing policy so that the price paid is fair as to not undermine the policy.

- Institute a policy that all drugs of any kind would be freely given to pharmaceutical companies for production of drugs and medicine. Any surplus would be destroyed.

- Institute a policy that anyone dealing with drugs outside of the official policy would face a mandatory jail sentence of at least ten years with no parole available.

Section XVIII –
Drinking Age

As most youth are intensely aware of, the national drinking age is twenty-one. I would like to think that this is just another one of the mistakes made over the years. What I really do not understand is this: any young man who is eighteen years old can enlist in the armed forces or, during times of draft, be conscripted. This young man can be sent to war anywhere in the world. In other words, he is old enough to go into combat and risk his life to protect our freedom. But when this young man comes home on leave, he cannot have an alcoholic beverage because he is underage. Does that make any sense? I think not.

Personally I do not drink and do not consider it a necessity, but it seems to me that if someone is old enough at eighteen to cast a vote or go to war, he should be old enough to have a drink or two. There are laws on the books now to deal with those who abuse the right, and new ones could be added if necessary. So in conclusion, we should either raise the voting age to twenty-one or lower the drinking age to eighteen and put some trust in our young men and women. Some may call this a trivial issue perhaps, but it is one that must have a commonsense solution.

SECTION XIX – TORT REFORM

Much has been said about the need to reform the health-care system, but nothing has been said about the high costs and some of the reasons behind them. It seems to me that just about all doctors want to double-check and triple-check before they start cutting, so to speak. Why is that? One of the reasons these expensive tests, such as X-rays, MRIs, and CT scans, are prescribed is the fear of lawsuits. Doctors in general must not only cover their overhead and make a profit; they also have to cover the insurance premium. Unfortunately, insurance premiums for adequate liability coverage have gone into the stratosphere. Some doctors, of course, have been found to be negligent, like in any other profession, but the vast majority strives to provide good care and they do. Nevertheless, the fear of a lawsuit hangs over their heads constantly. Lawyers do not help the situation; many will sue at the first chance or negotiate with a doctor's insurance carrier. The money involved is exorbitant and many get to be rich—many lawyers, I mean.

Our society has become somewhat litigious. We sue just because it is easy to do it. This practice of paying an attorney only if the case is won is ridiculous. There is no real effective system in place to screen frivolous suits and throw them out before they even start; therefore, the system favors the practitioners of law. Tort reform, if properly done, would be a tremendous asset to our economy and the welfare of all. When an individual or group pays astronomical fees, who do you think will actually be paying for that? All of us—in the form of higher prices. Just look and see what happened to the price of cigarettes in the last several years. I dream of seeing a system that mandates that anyone pursuing a lawsuit must pay his own lawyer even if he loses. The fee could be paid 50 percent up front and 50 percent before the start of the trial. No more contingency fee arrangements. I would love to see a cap on awards, and, in the case of major suits, I would like to do away with juries as they have a tendency to side with the underdog. A three-judge panel would hear and decide those cases.

SECTION XX –
THE ENGLISH LANGUAGE

The founding fathers wrote the Constitution in English. The Bill of Rights is written in English. Our laws are written in English. Why, then, are we afraid to proclaim that English is the American national language? I suspect the reason is political. I believe that none of our representatives in Washington today would dare offend a segment of the population whose native language is not English. I hear that some school systems demand that teachers know Spanish in order to qualify to teach. Do we really not see the damage being done? Does anyone care or is everyone interested in votes no matter where they come from?

I had an interesting experience some time ago. My wife and I were in a furniture store to get a few chairs. The store was in the Spanish-speaking section of the city. We went in and a nice, polite salesperson welcomed us. At first she spoke in Spanish, and when she realized we were not Spanish-speaking she tried English. Her English was very rough, and she had problems forming sentences or expressing herself. I tried to put her mind at ease by speaking a few words in Spanish and asking what her nationality was. She told us that she was Dominican. My wife then said that we had visited the Dominican Republic on vacation and had fallen in love with the people there. The saleslady was happy to hear that and said that she loved the place. I then asked how long she had been living here in the States. Her answer chilled me. She said that she was born here; she'd been born in the Bronx. She went to school in New York, and after roughly thirty years she could hardly communicate in English. We concluded the purchase and she was very happy, but the question I ask is, who was responsible for this young lady's education? Does anyone think that we are doing something good by not requiring they speak English in schools? This policy must end and give all children of foreign descent and background a chance to learn the language and be assimilated into our society.

All children, especially those of recent immigrants, must be taught the language properly and get a thorough education. Whatever language they speak at home will complement their cultural background, but while part of our society, they must communicate in the official language—English. Besides, what about other ethnic groups like Asians? We do not seem to be making the same allowances for them by holding classes in Tagalog or Chinese. They get ahead by adapting and learning quickly. Are we making assumptions that Spanish-speaking kids are not capable of learning the language? This would be incredibly foolish. They are as smart as they come and can overcome obstacles like anyone else. But first they need to be given the right tools, including fluency in the English language.

Section XXI – The States

All states must be ready to take charge of a new political process, the school system, the police system, the fire department, and the electoral process in their states.

The state political process must be overhauled like the federal system. Here, too, the Republican Party is one of the rich for the rich, and the Democrats might as well change the name of their party to the Socialist Party or Communist Party. Both have betrayed the silent and abused majority, so even here changes must come.

- The process for electing governors must mirror the process for electing the president. Primaries must take place at the same time as the election for president. Individuals would be allowed to contribute funds to the election campaign but corporations and businesses of all kinds, domestic or foreign, would not. Contribution could not exceed $5,000 per individual, and the maximum expenditure allowed in the primaries would be no more than $25,000,000 per candidate.

- Any candidate must be at least fifty (50) years of age and no more than sixty-five (65).

- The term served would be the same as the president of the United States—five (5) years per term with a maximum of two (2) terms or ten (10) years.

- The compensation for governors would be left up to the state legislatures; however, all governors would be part of the Social Security system for retirement benefits.

- At the primaries the candidates would be selected by the same process as for the federal election. At that point the states would finance the candidates with state funds in the amount of $30,000,000 per candidate. The same federal rules would apply to states, and no other contribution of money, goods, or services, including free advertising, would be allowed. Violation of these rules would automatically disqualify a candidate.

- The governor would be the commander in chief of the state National Guard, the state police, which would replace all local police forces, and the fire department.

- The governor would have a lieutenant governor, who would take over the governor's job in the event of death or incapacitation. The president of the state senate would take over in the event that both the governor and lieutenant governor were unable to serve.

- If the senate president were to take over the office of the governor, the senate would elect a new senate president.

Section XXII –
The State Senate

The new state senate would be a combination of the existing state legislative bodies. This would be done, not only to streamline the legislative process, but also to save a bundle of money in the process, which could be put to better use. So first merge the two houses and create a new entity of no more than fifty senators, possibly fewer.

- To be eligible to be a state senator, one must be forty (40) years of age and no older than sixty-five (65).

- State senators would serve for a maximum of ten (10) years or two five (5) year terms.

- Election of state senators would be staggered so as to have new members come in every couple of years.

- The new senate would consider bills individually, without attachments or riders. Each bill would be considered on its merit.

- The new senate would debate and approve all budgets; however, the governor would have line-item veto power.

- The governor could veto any bill, and the senate would need at least 60 percent of the votes to override the veto.

- The new senate would elect its own president right after the election results are ratified and the new senate is in. The senate president would cast a tie-breaking vote in the event of a tie.

- Senators must cast a vote. No abstentions and no "present" votes are allowed. Three abstentions in the course of anyone's term would result in expulsion from the senate.

- The new senate would have the responsibility to confirm or reject any justices named for the state supreme court. Any and all justices named for the post would have to be voted on unless he or she withdraws from nomination.

Section XXIII –
The State Supreme Court

The state supreme court justices would be named for one ten (10) year term. Here, too, we need continuous, smooth turnover, so the terms would be staggered so as to see a new justice every couple of years.

- To be eligible, one must be at least fifty-five (55) years old and no older than sixty-five (65).

- One must have been a judge in some capacity for at least ten (10) years.

- One must have a been a resident of the state for at least ten (10) years.

- One must not have any criminal record or have been subject to any criminal investigation for any reason, no matter what the outcome was.

- Justices must apply the law and not legislate from the bench. A judicial review board would monitor decisions and determine if the law was applied or not and recommend actions.

- The state supreme court would hear all cases brought before it and not be selective.

Section XXIV –
The Education System

The topic of the school system has been beaten to death with no real tangible results. The system is broken and there is no will to fix it. The system is highly discriminatory and must be corrected so that everyone has a chance at getting a good education, the lack of which has been a component of some of the problems we have been facing for years. It seems to me that a segment of our society likes things the way they are. This minority wants to keep control of the politics of the country, and it suits them fine to keep other segments of the general population where they are. In this instance we should take a good hard look at what other countries are doing and, if it appears to be working, shamelessly copy some of their techniques. I have heard as you may have, that the mind is a great gift; let's not see it go to waste. Let's stop the empty talk and take action, as education, or lack of it, may be the issue that is going to sink this country. All kids must have an equal chance at getting a good education, as some of these kids will be our leaders in the future.

When I look at my real estate tax bill, I see that a good chunk of what I pay goes to support the local school system. Every city and town does the same thing. Each community must educate the kids of their residents. This creates education systems with different standards and objectives. Those communities that have wealthy residents who can afford to pay high real estate taxes have school systems with just about everything educators dream about: good teachers, good equipment, and no worry as to where the money is coming from. Typically these communities see a high percentage of their students pursue a higher education while the poor communities never get out from under. This is what I call discrimination against middle-to-low-income families. These communities are filled with people who struggle to make a living and do not see any chance of watching their kids make something of themselves. Yes, you hear that once in while some kids really excel, and they cannot be ignored, but those are rare exceptions. That's why they end up in the headlines: they've done the unexpected.

The new education system must be equitable and must be devoid of any racial preferences, as these preferences do more damage to the kids than anyone cares to discuss. I am not sure about the time, but about twenty-five years ago the Jersey City Board of Education got slapped with a lawsuit.

The action was brought by an African American young man who contended that the school was negligent in giving him a diploma. After he graduated he could not even fill out an application for employment. This event was reported by the *Wall Street Journal* at the time. I do not know what happened to the suit, but a lesson must be learned from it. What good is it to push kids forward when they are not ready? Everyone agrees that the school systems are impregnated with local politics, something that must be taken out of the system.

For starters I dream of seeing a uniform school system in each and every state. I dream of seeing each state take over the education system and mandate that each and every community follow the same curriculum with just a few elective subjects available to all students.

I dream of seeing the kids in the wealthy communities receive the same education as those in the poor neighborhoods. To achieve that, teachers must first be compensated adequately so as to attract good people to the profession. They must be given the skills and the authority to teach our kids.

When teachers are second-guessed by the politics, the ones who suffer are the kids. That must stop.

I do not want to see teachers abuse our kids, but I do not want to see them threatened with lawsuits if they try to discipline anyone. Parents, too, must bear some responsibility and must be supportive of all teaching staff.

The new system would allow each state to have private and parochial schools of some kind or another; however, each school must adhere to the same curriculum requirements that state schools go by.

Each and every school must be subject to state inspections, and teachers must be held accountable. Any teachers that do not meet the bare minimum requirement must be retrained and, if that fails, replaced.

I dream of a demanding system but a fair one to all. I want to see our kids and grandkids grow to be ambitious and smart and backed with a good education. I want to see the state produce the kind of education that only ivy league schools do right now. We need the kind of universities that anyone can access and that will produce good professionals of all kinds.

In summary here is what I envision:

- State-run schools financed by a state tax while the local real estate tax would be eliminated. Fifty percent would be contributed by the federal government.

- The state would run all schools from kindergarten to PhD programs.

- All existing schools currently managed by the cities and towns and their infrastructure would be absorbed by the states.

- The state secretary of education would hold a cabinet post and would be accountable to the legislature and the governor.

- The management of the system would have to be well structured to provide the needed support without interfering with the teaching.

- College tuition would be a nominal amount. Primary education and high school would still be free. State universities would be paid tuition of approximately $3,000 per year regardless of how many courses one takes.

- The admission tests would be eliminated, and anyone completing high school, who wishes to do so, could enroll in a higher education program. This would be a sink or swim program.

- While entering a state university might be easy, getting a degree would be contingent on one's work and not on the ethnicity of anyone. Students who work hard and do the work would be bestowed the much-wanted degree.

- Teachers would be paid a salary commensurate with their experience and tenure, but it would be a living salary so as to attract the best of the best. Our kids and grandkids deserve it.

- Teachers would have to go for periodic training and make sure their skills are not compromised by the passage of time.

- Teachers would not be allowed to introduce politics in the classrooms until high school. Let the minds of the kids develop without any interference.

- There would be mandatory periodic testing of the kids, once at the end of primary school and twice in high school. The first high school examination would be after the second year and the second, at the end of the fourth year.

- Students would be allowed to fail a grade and, if necessary, repeat the year. No point in pushing anyone forward if he or she is not ready.

- In this system no preference would be given to any ethnic group. Everyone would have to meet the exact same requirements in order to graduate.

- The national requirements would be established by the state board of education, which would operate within the Department of Education and would be reviewed frequently.

- Under the secretary of education superintendents, deans, assistants, principals, and other personnel will help fulfill the smaller duties so that the system is followed and the individual schools are not compromised.

- Discipline will be taught on a regular basis with the help of the parents.

- Teachers who do not meet the criteria or the follow-up testing would be replaced.

- Teachers would be part of the Social Security system that would guarantee a decent retirement.

- Classes would have no more than thirty students, no matter what. When possible, there would be fewer than thirty students per teacher so as to ensure they get the proper attention.

SECTION XXV –
THE STATE POLICE DEPARTMENT

What we have today is a system that perhaps was appropriate in the post-Revolution times, when each community had to take care of itself and protect its residents. Times have changed and we need something better. Just look at some of the situations we have had over the years. We may have a mayor who does not agree with state or federal laws so he orders his police department not to enforce those particular laws. We have police departments in small communities that do not have enough funds to buy equipment or, in some instances, even the gas to power their cars. Here, too, it seems to me that some discrimination exists. Again those communities with wealth can get what they want, and those less fortunate will get less than the bare minimum. Are the citizens of poor communities deserving less protection and services from their police department than those living in rich cities and towns? I think not. Hence the need to revamp and update the system.

I recommend that all police departments in all communities be taken over by a brand-new state police department under the direct management of the governor. Policemen would be working for the state and getting paid by the state. This would ensure that all communities would have the services needed, regardless of their own financial situation. The entire department would be headed by the state secretary of internal security. This would be a cabinet post, under which one would find a chain of command as we have today, but the chain of command would be streamlined across the state. We would have the same uniforms for all and a code of conduct for everyone wearing a badge.

This system would be financed by the state, which would increase state taxes; however, the city and town taxes would see a drastic decrease because no police financing would be necessary at the local level. Only the state police would be allowed to carry weapons. The cities could have traffic police, enforcement for meter payment, and some administrative personnel, but these people would not carry guns, let alone use them.

In summary we will carry out the following:

- A consolidation of all police departments under the state.

- A police structure that allows the various departments to operate under uniform guidelines but with some autonomy.

- All management officers would be held to the same standards and would be accountable for their actions.

- The police force would have branches within, such as highway patrols, undercover agents, detectives, etc. These posts would be filled essentially by the same people holding those positions now.

- The level of pay would be standardized so that a police officer working in a big city would not make a lot more than an officer in a small city except for some variance due to the cost of living difference.

- Policemen would be compensated so as to make a decent living and would be part of the Social Security system for retirement benefits.

Section XXVI – Cities and Towns

We all have heard about a few mayors who crowned themselves as emperors of their cities. These public servants have proclaimed to themselves and their cronies that they are above the law—not just city ordinances but also state and federal laws. They have made a mockery of our judicial system with their accomplices at the state houses and in Washington as well. For the last four decades I have heard time and again that we are a nation of laws. However, laws do not seem to apply to some people, who unfortunately have been able to get away with that. Why do you think these mayors defy the law? Certainly not for the benefit of the citizens. Rather, they have been appealing to certain segments of the voting population who have the ability to help with their aspirations to higher office. If unchecked, they will certainly succeed. Hence the urgent need to alter the duties and responsibilities of mayors and city managers all around the country.

Mayors in general should only be "city administrators," responsible for a city's administrative duties. Under the new system mayors would no longer be in charge of the police department, the fire department, or the school system because these would be part of a state-wide system.

All cities would be responsible for, but not limited to, the following. Some cities, due to their size, might have different issues, which can be dealt with independent of the state.

- City charters will be amended to reduce the responsibilities of mayors.

- To be eligible for the position of mayor, one must be at least forty (40) years of age and no older than sixty-five (65).

- Mayors would be eligible to hold office for two terms only, and terms would last five years.

- No one with a criminal record of any kind would be eligible.

- The candidate with the most votes would be declared the winner of the election, and the individual would then serve for five years.

- City and town responsibilities would include the following: traffic police, parking law enforcement, support of parks and recreation centers, and building and city infrastructure maintenance. The city would be responsible for funding all projects it wants with some assistance from the state and the federal government. In short, the city would have to pay 50 percent of the cost; the state, 30 percent; and the federal government, 20 percent. This would avoid any waste and do away with the so-called pork projects. If something is needed, then the city must raise the funds necessary.

Mayors would be city administrators and would keep away from state or national politics. The people need civil servants who work for them and not the other way around; they certainly do not need people who intend to use the city merely as a springboard for their political ambitions.

SECTION XXVII – THE CITY COUNCILS

City councils in a lot of cases put a rubber stamp on whatever the mayor wants. That must change, and it will change with the advent of our new party. I've seen and heard that for starters, some who run for council's office do it for their ego or because they are part of a clique and must be taken care of or because they want to do something with their time. In short there is not real commitment to serve the people and what is right for their cities. That must change. People who feel they have a civic responsibility to fulfill must run for office under our new banner. They must push forth programs that will reform the management of the cities, eliminate waste, eliminate corruption, and if necessary act to remove the mayor if he or she violates laws, state or federal. To be eligible to run for council's office one must:

- Be at least forty (40) years of age and no older than sixty-five (65).

- Have a minimum of a high school diploma.

- Have been a resident of the city for at least five years.

- Be a U.S. citizen or naturalized citizen.

- Be clear of any criminal record of any kind. In the event the official is convicted of any crime, be it a misdemeanor or a felony, he or she would be expelled, and a special election would be held to select a replacement.

The following changes will also be made.

- Officials will serve no more than two terms of five years each.

- The role of the council would be much more open and responsible than it appears to be today, when one hardly hears about anything that they are doing. They are not there to rubber stamp what the mayor wants. Instead, they will pursue their own projects and report to the public frequently.

Section XXVIII –
The Municipal Taxation System

Now that cities and towns do not have the burden of the school system, the police department, or the fire department, they will need a lot less funds than they do today. They can still have real estate taxes, but they must be calibrated so the city will generate only the funds necessary to manage its affairs. In short the taxes must be revised to exclude the following:

- School tax

- Police department tax

- Fire department tax

- Municipal courts (which will also be absorbed by the state)

The taxes should still support the following:

- Sewage treatment

- Parks and recreation

- City maintenance

- Traffic management

- Tourist information centers

I envision a tax cut by the cities of about 65 percent or more.

Section XXIX –
Municipal Services

Once the cities and town are patrolled by the state police, and the fire departments are under state management, what are the cities and towns responsible for?

- Building and maintaining all infrastructure within the city limits.

- Building and maintaining all parks and playgrounds.

- Building and maintaining educational structures such as zoos or aquariums.

- Maintaining and directing an adequate traffic and parking enforcement system.

- Building and maintaining sewer systems and water systems.

- Enforcing zoning laws as passed by the city council.

- Coordinating with state police and state fire marshals to provide assistance in the event of problems.

In conclusion, together with collective actions we can take our country back from the claws of special interest groups and corrupt politicians. Let us restore this beautiful, tired, maligned country to what it once was. God bless the U.S.A. and all of its citizens.